Conquering Procrastination
Habit-based Strategies for Ultimate Efficiency

Benedict H. Clark

Table of Contents

1. Introduction 2
2. Understanding Procrastination: A Comprehensive Breakdown ... 3
   - 2.1. The Anatomy of Procrastination 3
   - 2.2. Unraveling the Relationship: Procrastination and Emotions .. 3
   - 2.3. The Factors that Fuel Procrastination 4
   - 2.4. The Pervasiveness of Procrastination: A Societal Issue? ... 5
   - 2.5. The Negative Impacts of Procrastination 5
3. Peering into the Mind: The Psychology of Procrastination ... 6
   - 3.1. The Cognitive Paradigm 6
   - 3.2. The Emotional Underpinnings 7
   - 3.3. Interplay of Time Perception 7
   - 3.4. Procrastination: An Evolutionary Perspective 8
4. Time: Your Most Underrated Resource 9
   - 4.1. Identifying the Value of Time 9
   - 4.2. Dispelling the Illusion of Abundant Time 9
   - 4.3. The Role of Time Perception in Productivity 10
   - 4.4. Techniques for Time Management 10
   - 4.5. The Temporal Nature of Habits 10
   - 4.6. Redeeming Wasted Time: It's Never Too Late 11
5. The Dynamics of Habit Formation: Inside the Human Behavior .. 12
   - 5.1. Conscious vs. Subconscious Mind 12
   - 5.2. Behavioral Triggers 13
   - 5.3. Habit Loop 13
   - 5.4. Antecedents, Behaviors, and Consequences 14
   - 5.5. Changing Habits 14
6. Procrastination to Productivity: The Habit Shift 16
   - 6.1. Reframing our Understanding of Habits 16
   - 6.2. Habit Loop: The Three R's 16

- 6.3. Systems over Goals: A New Perspective … 17
- 6.4. Habit Stacking: Harnessing Existing Habits … 18
- 6.5. Overcoming Procrastination: Making the Habit Shift … 18
- 7. Employing Behavioral Techniques for Procrastination … 20
  - 7.1. The Foundation of Behavioral Techniques … 20
  - 7.2. The Power of Positive Reinforcement … 20
  - 7.3. Negative Reinforcement and Procrastination … 21
  - 7.4. The Role of Punishment in Behavior Modification … 21
  - 7.5. Employing Behavioral Techniques for Long-Term Change … 22
- 8. Maximizing Time Management: Tools and Techniques … 24
  - 8.1. The Principle of Time Boxing … 24
  - 8.2. The Power of Breaks: The Pomodoro Technique … 24
  - 8.3. Prioritizing with Pareto Principle and Eisenhower Box … 25
  - 8.4. Embracing Technology: Digital Tools and Applications … 25
  - 8.5. Mindful Living: Meditation, Exercise, and Healthy Eating … 26
- 9. Becoming an Efficiency Expert: Practical Approaches … 27
  - 9.1. Deconstructing Tasks into Manageable Units … 27
  - 9.2. Harnessing the Power of Technology … 28
  - 9.3. Prioritizing Tasks Effectively … 28
  - 9.4. Adopting Effective Time Management Techniques … 29
  - 9.5. Developing and Maintaining a Positive Mindset … 29
  - 9.6. Creating a Conducive Work Environment … 30
- 10. Maintaining Productivity Momentum: Avoiding Backslide … 31
  - 10.1. The Concept and Importance of Momentum … 31
  - 10.2. Strategies to Keep the Momentum Going … 32
    - 10.2.1. Positive Reinforcement … 32
    - 10.2.2. Regular Evaluation and Tracking Your Progress … 32
    - 10.2.3. Adopt A Growth Mindset … 32
    - 10.2.4. Taking Purposeful Breaks … 33
    - 10.2.5. Seek Feedback … 33

10.3. Bouncing Back from Slip-ups: The Art of Resilience 33
11. Turning a New Leaf: Your Future Free of Procrastination 35
    11.1. Nurturing the Productivity Powerhouse 35
    11.2. Cultivating Resilience Amidst Setbacks 36
    11.3. Guarding Against Procrastination Relapse 36
    11.4. The Power of Consistency 36
    11.5. Embracing Agility: Adapting Your Strategies 36
    11.6. Envisioning a Procrastination-Free Future 37

Procrastination is the bad habit of putting off until the day after tomorrow what should have been done the day before yesterday.

— Napoleon Hill

Chapter 1. Introduction

Unveiling our groundbreaking Special Report: "Conquering Procrastination: Habit-based Strategies for Ultimate Efficiency." Imagine what life would look like if you could wave goodbye to the perpetual cycle of stress, missed deadlines, and guilt that often comes packaged with that all too familiar foe: procrastination. This compelling report is your ticket to reclaim your time, increase your productivity, and live life on your own terms! Bursting with proven, actionable strategies, our report invites readers into a world where time is no longer an enemy, but an ally. The transformation into a productivity powerhouse is not just possible - it's within your reach! So, why wait another minute? The power to conquer procrastination, refine your habits, and unveil unmatched efficiency awaits. Embrace the journey and rekindle your relationship with time today with our illuminating special report.

Chapter 2. Understanding Procrastination: A Comprehensive Breakdown

Understanding procrastination is the critical first step in defeating it. It's much more than a simple character flaw, but rather, a complex interchange of cognitive and behavioral components influenced by different aspects. Let's dive in with a detailed analysis and comprehensive breakdown of procrastination.

2.1. The Anatomy of Procrastination

There are various ways to approach the understanding of procrastination. Although it might appear as a mere habit of delaying tasks, it has a deeper psychological basis. Broadly speaking, procrastination is the voluntary delay of an intended course of action despite knowing that this delay may lead to unfavorable outcomes. It is not just about laziness, but can also be rooted in issues around self-esteem, fear of failure, or excessive perfectionism.

What makes procrastination fascinating is its paradoxical nature. People are consciously choosing to delay tasks, fully aware of the potential negative impact. Yet, they are unable to stop themselves. This illogical behaviour points to a disconnect between intention and action, a defining hallmark of procrastination.

2.2. Unraveling the Relationship: Procrastination and Emotions

Understanding the relationship between procrastination and emotions is vital to grasp the overall picture. Some psychologists argue that procrastination is more about our incapacity to manage negative moods or emotional distress related to a task, a theory known as temporal motivation theory. It suggests that we are biased towards the immediate relief that procrastination offers against feelings of anxiety, boredom or insecurity related to the task, temporarily ignoring the long-term consequences.

Another critical way emotions become involved is through the cycle of self-blame, guilt, and regret that follows procrastination. With each repeated procrastination episode, this cycle deepens, reinforcing the self-image of being a "procrastinator."

2.3. The Factors that Fuel Procrastination

There are three intertwined factors that fuel procrastination: Behavioral avoidance, cognitive distortion, and maladaptive beliefs.

1. Behavioral avoidance: This represents the desire to avoid discomfort, whether it be the discomfort of a challenging task or - more often - the discomfort of difficult emotions associated with the task.
2. Cognitive distortion: These are irrational beliefs about oneself and the world, such as overestimating the time left for work, underestimating the time required for tasks, or the illusion that future self will be more equipped to handle the task.
3. Maladaptive beliefs: Procrastinators often harbor maladaptive beliefs relating to their self-esteem or self-efficacy, such as a fear of failure or success, perfectionistic standards, or debilitating self-doubt.

Understanding these drivers can equip one with a more targeted approach towards overcoming procrastination.

2.4. The Pervasiveness of Procrastination: A Societal Issue?

Recent research has suggested that a staggering 15-20% of adults and 50% of students procrastinate regularly, suggesting a societal influence on the widespread nature of procrastination. This could be attributed to our increasingly fast-paced lifestyles, where long-term goals often get overlooked in favor of immediate pleasures or more pressing demands. The rise of distractions, such as smartphones and social media, also aid in fuelling procrastination.

2.5. The Negative Impacts of Procrastination

While the short term impacts of procrastination include stress and rushed work leading to poor quality, the long term consequences are more severe. Chronic procrastinators may experience harmful effects on their mental health, including heightened anxiety, depression, and low self-esteem. Long term procrastination also harms one's physical health through increased stress and neglect of health-promoting behaviours like exercise or doctor appointments.

In conclusion, understanding procrastination requires analysis from a wide spectrum. It's not just a time management issue but a multifaceted, complex problem that requires a deep dive into one's psychological, emotional, and behavioural aspects. A true comprehension of procrastination and its effects can reveal insights into coping mechanisms, setting the stage for effective strategies to increase productivity and overall life satisfaction.

After all, as George Ainsley once said, "Procrastination is not laziness, but a considerable failure of self-regulation." Understanding it is the first step towards changing that dynamic.

Chapter 3. Peering into the Mind: The Psychology of Procrastination

Delving into the human mind is akin to navigating an intriguing labyrinth. Understanding the psychological roots of procrastination requires a similarly extensive exploration of the complex depths of human cognition, emotion, and behavior. It behooves us to consider procrastination not as an isolated nuisance but as a subtle reflection of our internal mental processes.

3.1. The Cognitive Paradigm

The cognitive aspect of procrastination is paramount in comprehending this widespread phenomenon. A core component of this perspective is an understanding of how one's thought processes can either spur or impede action. The spotlight often falls on negative cognitive patterns, such as perfectionism, fear of failure, and self-deprecating thoughts. These patterns, deeply entrenched in one's psyche, can foster a self-fulfilling prophecy where procrastination is both a symptom and a cause of further distress.

Take, for example, perfectionism. This cognitive outlook, often steeped in societal expectations, propels one in a ceaseless search for unattainable perfection. The fear of delivering subpar work can be debilitating and can easily breed procrastination. The self-preserving decision to avoid failure may, ironically, prevent one from fulfilling tasks to their potential, thus contributing to a spiraling effect of procrastination and disappointing results.

3.2. The Emotional Underpinnings

Emotion and cognition are inextricably linked, shaping the landscape for human behavior including procrastination. To a considerable extent, procrastination can be viewed as an escape mechanism, a psychological refuge from uncomfortable emotions or from tasks that provoke such feelings.

Anxiety, for instance, has a notorious reputation for being a bedfellow of procrastination. Stressful tasks can trigger anxiety, leading to avoidance behaviors as a means to manage acute emotional distress. But here's the rub: the more one avoids the task, the more anxiety intensifies. This forms a vicious circle of anxiety and procrastination that can be challenging to break.

Similarly, tasks deemed boring or uninteresting can invoke feelings of restlessness or irritability. Procrastination, then, becomes a tool to delay the onset of such unwelcome feelings, indicating an underlying emotional regulation strategy.

3.3. Interplay of Time Perception

Weaving together the fabric of cognition and emotion is our perception of time. Procrastination is nestled within the interplay of our interpretations of the present and the future.

Procrastinators are often said to possess a "present bias," where the allure of immediate gratification takes precedence over long-term rewards. Dividing an intimidating project into manageable chunks, or associating unpleasant tasks with delayed, but larger, benefits helps to cognitive reorientation towards future rewards and thus reduces procrastination.

3.4. Procrastination: An Evolutionary Perspective

A more intriguing dimension in our exploration of procrastination is viewing it through the evolutionary lens. One could argue that early humans—our ancestors—procrastinated in situations where immediate action did not confer survival benefits. Similarly, in the modern context, our tendencies to procrastinate could be remnants of this evolutionary past.

Akin to our ancestors who perfectly calibrated their energy expenditure, we may also subconsciously decide to procrastinate to conserve energy for other tasks deemed more crucial to our well-being. This perspective urges us to view procrastination not solely as a detrimental trait but as a potential adaptation that requires cautious harnessing.

In sum, peering into the mind and drawing out the psychological patterns that fuel procrastination is a captivating endeavor. From cognitive tendencies and emotional regulation strategies to skewed perceptions of time and potential evolutionary roots, procrastination emerges as a multidimensional phenomenon. These insights deliver the foundation for transforming this understanding into tangible strategies for overcoming procrastination, which we will explore in the chapters that follow.

Chapter 4. Time: Your Most Underrated Resource

Every second that you breathe, every tick of the clock, is a moment moving forward in the grand scheme of time. Countless individuals have realized that time, although intangible, is perhaps the most vital resource one has at their disposal. Nonetheless, it remains one of the most underrated components in our everyday lives.

4.1. Identifying the Value of Time

Despite the saying that time is money, in reality, time is immeasurably more valuable. Money, after all, can be earned back - but time, once gone, is irretrievable. The failure to recognize the worth of time underlies procrastination, which begets the vicious cycle of delayed tasks and accumulated stress. It is important to highlight that time's scarcity intensifies its value. This isn't about scaremongering; it's about adopting a realistic perspective on the brevity and value of our most fleeting, non-renewable resource.

4.2. Dispelling the Illusion of Abundant Time

To wield time effectively, one must first shatter the illusion that there is an abundance of it. Procrastinators often persuade themselves, "I'll do it tomorrow," failing to realize that tomorrow is never guaranteed and that today's procrastination leads to tomorrow's backlog. Understanding that time perpetually slips away can propel one to take immediate action, curbing procrastination at its roots.

4.3. The Role of Time Perception in Productivity

Notably, our perception of time governs our productivity. A skewed or distorted view leads us to overestimate or underestimate the duration we need for tasks, leading to inefficiencies and delays. Consequently, harnessing a more accurate awareness of time is key to defeating procrastination. Through techniques like time tracking and time blocking, one can realistically gauge the time required for tasks, thereby eliminating surprises and minimizing the phenomenon of time scarcity.

4.4. Techniques for Time Management

Here we delve into a battery of techniques that aim to refine your management of time:

Practice mindfulness: Mindfulness keeps one aware of the present moment, thereby enhancing focus on the task at hand. This reduces the chances of getting diverted, ensuring that time is well-spent.

It's important to remember that these techniques aren't one-size-fits-all solutions. One must experiment and figure out the mix of strategies that work best for their lifestyle, routine, and work nature.

4.5. The Temporal Nature of Habits

Our habits, both beneficial and detrimental, exist in the temporal realm. They follow a cue, routine, and reward structure, contained within a specific temporal boundary. Consequently, the formation and modification of habits become a matter of adjusting our relationship with time.

For instance, replacing procrastination - a negative habit - with productivity requires a change not only in perception, but also in time usage. Habits shape and are shaped by our allocation of time. When we cease to view time as an infinite, expendable resource, we become more meticulous in choosing which habits will take up that time.

4.6. Redeeming Wasted Time: It's Never Too Late

The feeling of having lost or wasted time can be disheartening. However, it's essential to remember that it's never too late for change. The human brain is highly adaptable; it can learn and unlearn behaviors, even those that are deeply ingrained. Each moment providing an opportunity for improvement, the journey towards effective time management and improved productivity remains ever accessible.

In conclusion, recognizing time as our most underrated resource is pivotal to conquering procrastination. By developing a profound respect and understanding of time, by employing and personalizing various time management strategies, and by modifying our habits to reflect this awareness, we can gradually alleviate the struggle of procrastination. Remember, every tick of the clock is an invitation: an invitation to act, to change, to become a better version of ourselves. Embrace this invitation, and transform your relationship with time to live a more efficient, productive life.

Chapter 5. The Dynamics of Habit Formation: Inside the Human Behavior

It is essential to look at the very roots of human behavior to understand the driving force behind our habits. This exploration includes the constant dance between our conscious and subconscious minds, our environment's influence, emergency behaviors shaped by our survival instincts, and the myriad of other factors that play a part in shaping our habits and subsequently, our lives.

5.1. Conscious vs. Subconscious Mind

Understanding the dynamics of our conscious and subconscious minds is the first step on this intricate journey. Our conscious mind is responsible for our thoughts, actions, and feelings that we're aware of in any given moment. Our conscious mind is like a spotlight we shine only on select parts of our experiences. On the other hand, our subconscious mind holds an immense amount of information we're not actively thinking about, including our underlying beliefs, experiences, and impulses.

Our subconscious mind is like a vast storage room, holding everything not in the spotlight. It is this subconscious faculty that is responsible for driving a lot of our habitual behaviors. Our habits, formed and reinforced over time, reside in the subconscious mind. They are automatic routines that save us time and cognitive energy.

5.2. Behavioral Triggers

The cornerstone of habit formation lies in identifying behavioral triggers. These triggers indicate when a particular habit should occur. They are specific signals that our brain has associated with a given habit. Triggers can be external, like a particular location, time of the day, certain people, or a specific event. They can also be internal, such as a particular feeling, thought, or physiological state.

For example, the simple act of waking up in the morning (external trigger) may trigger the habit of brushing your teeth (behavior). An internal sensation like hunger (internal trigger) might prompt you to start cooking or order food (behavior). Essentially, triggers provide vital locational information for where a habit lives in your daily routine.

5.3. Habit Loop

Central to the science of habit formation is Charles Duhigg's concept of the 'Habit Loop.' This is a continuous, three-part loop that includes the cue (trigger), routine (behavior), and reward. The cue or trigger acts as the catalyst, prompting the routine, which follows inevitably unless interrupted. The reward signals to the brain that the routine was beneficial.

This system operates as a feedback loop, learning and improving with each repetition of the cycle. Eventually, the connection between cue and routine becomes so strong that it's almost automatic - that's when a habit is formed. And remember, habits aren't restricted to physical behaviors; thought patterns and emotional responses can become habits too.

5.4. Antecedents, Behaviors, and Consequences

Building on the Habit Loop concept, is the ABC's of behavior – Antecedents (like triggers or cues), Behaviors, and Consequences. Antecedents precede the behavior, and their interpretation subsequently leads to certain behaviors. Consequences follow the behavior and influence future actions. Essentially, individuals learn to associate certain consequences (either positive or negative) with particular behaviors and antecedents.

For instance, given the antecedent of 'stress,' the behavior might be 'scrolling social media,' which yields the immediate consequence of 'temporary relief.' This may cause the behavior to be repeated in the future when the stress pops up again since the brain has learned to associate relief with this behavior. This understanding of ABC can be used to decrease detrimental habits and enhance beneficial ones.

5.5. Changing Habits

Knowing the ways of persistent bad habits is only half the battle; transformation lies in changing those habits. This could be done by replacing the bad behaviors with good ones, infusing the rewards into new practices or reshaping your environment making it conducive to the new behavior you want to adopt.

Considering our old example of using social media under stress, a new, healthier habit might be picking up a book instead. Although the antecedent (stress) remains the same, the behavior changes, and so do the consequences. Now the relief is paired with a sense of accomplishment and learning rather than the short-lived pacification which social media scrolling brings.

As humans, we are wired to strive for efficiency. Therefore, the formation of habits is a natural inclination of our beings, a way for our mind to settle into a 'low power mode' by turning day-to-day actions into routines. Understanding this dynamic can play a significant role in forming and changing our habits, ultimately paving the way for better work efficiency and health.

It is essential to remember that habit formation is a timely process that operates at a varying pace for different individuals. Leaping into productive habits requires steady, gradual progress, tolerance, and patience with oneself. The transformation can be challenging but remember: it's not just about the destination, but also about the journey of self-growth and self-betterment.

Chapter 6. Procrastination to Productivity: The Habit Shift

The transformation from procrastination to productivity doesn't emerge instantaneously, nor is it a journey without obstacles. Nevertheless, by utilizing the robust tools of habit formation and modification, one can gradually make this shift and cultivate a harmonious relationship with time and productivity. This chapter unveils actionable insights to transition from the passivity of procrastination to the dynamic realm of productivity using the power of habits.

6.1. Reframing our Understanding of Habits

Before diving into the habit shift, it is vital to elaborate on our understanding of habits. As consistent and repetitive pattern of behaviors, they emerge unconsciously through consistent repetition, forming the backbone of our everyday life. While habits often have a reputation for being difficult to change, they are malleable, given the right approach and circumstances.

6.2. Habit Loop: The Three R's

The framework of the habit loop, posited by Charles Duhigg in his book "The Power of Habit," is key to understanding how to alter our habits. This loop includes three components: the Cue (or Reminder), Routine, and Reward. Together, these elements offer a systematic manner of evaluating and eventually modifying our habits.

The Cue or Reminder is the trigger that initiates the habit. This could be time, location, emotional state, other people, or the preceding action. In the context of procrastination, a trigger could be the overwhelming size of a task or a feeling of discomfort associated with it.

The Routine constitutes the behavior itself—the act of procrastinating. This could encompass distractions such as social media scrolling, watching TV instead of working, or even household chores that suddenly become more appealing when a due date approaches.

Finally, the Reward is the immediate gratification that follows the routine. Often, this is relief from the discomfort or anxiety the task might cause.

To transition from procrastination to productivity, understanding your individual habit loop becomes crucial. Identifying the components of your procrastination habit loop can be the first proactive step towards transformation.

6.3. Systems over Goals: A New Perspective

While setting goals is a popular productivity strategy, researching habit change reveals a different narrative. We often set grand, ambitious goals as the antidote to procrastination, but the goals alone don't instigate change. This is where systems come into play.

In contrast to goals, systems focus on the process rather than the end result. A goal might be to write a book, but the system is committing to 500 words per day. To achieve productivity, we need to change our habits—the minute-to-minute actions—not merely the outcomes.

Drawing from this, by adopting systems, one can facilitate baby steps to conquer procrastination. Whether you're a writer aiming to write a thousand words daily or an athlete intending to train for two hours each morning, outlining systems—consistent, actionable routines—brings the long-term goal within reach.

6.4. Habit Stacking: Harnessing Existing Habits

Developed by BJ Fogg, a psychologist and researcher at Stanford, habit stacking can be a highly-effective tool for individuals seeking to instill new productive habits into their lives. Habit stacking involves inserting a new habit into the existing web of your daily activities. By tying the new behavior directly to a pre-existing habit, you can smoothly integrate it into your routine.

The concept arises from the notion that it's much easier to build upon habits we've already ingrained into our lives. So, if your aim is to spend more time reading, you could stack this new habit onto an existing one, such as drinking your morning coffee. This way, the established habit of enjoying coffee serves as a trigger for the new routine of reading, which further amplifies and sustains your productivity.

6.5. Overcoming Procrastination: Making the Habit Shift

The shift from procrastination to productivity necessitates a two-pronged approach. On one hand, it is about curating new, productive habits using tools such as systems and habit stacking. On the other hand, it involves altering pre-existing procrastination habits using the habit loop.

The key is to remember that patience, consistency, and gentle self-compassion are crucial during this transitional phase. After all, you are not only contending against procrastination but also orchestrating a significant cognitive and behavioral metamorphosis.

Don't rush the process, instead celebrate small wins and incremental progress.

In closing, it's clear that the battle with procrastination isn't one to be won overnight, but with continual, conscious behavior change, you can become the architect of your productivity. Harness the power of habits to shift from procrastination to productivity and re-establish a balanced, harmonious relationship with your time.

Chapter 7. Employing Behavioral Techniques for Procrastination

In this distinct chapter, we delve into the realm of behavioral modifications and the core strategies that you can deploy to effectively tackle procrastination. To understand the ins and outs of these techniques, it's crucial to first appreciate the premise they are built upon.

7.1. The Foundation of Behavioral Techniques

Behavioral techniques fundamentally revolve around our understanding and manipulation of human behavior. This realm of psychology is steeped in the belief that all behaviors are either acquired through conditioning or are a consequence of our interactions with the surrounding environment. Successful behavior modification therefore involves a blend of manipulating environmental cues and incentivizing desirable behaviors while simultaneously discouraging undesired ones. By mastering and implementing these techniques, you can foster the growth of productivity-enhancing habits and sideline the influence of procrastination.

7.2. The Power of Positive Reinforcement

When approached correctly, positive reinforcement can be an incredibly effective tool in your fight against procrastination. In essence, this method involves providing a rewarding stimulus following a certain behavior, thereby increasing the likelihood of that behavior being repeated in the future.

For example, after completing a demanding task that you've been postponing, treat yourself to a well-deserved break, an episode of your favorite series, or a small snack. By doing so, you effectively associate the completion of a task with a reward, thus making future tasks enticing.

However, it's important to strike a balance with positive reinforcement. Think of it as a delicate art rather than a brute force tactic. It's critical to ensure the rewards don't become the sole focus, but rather serve as a complimentary pat on the back for embracing productivity and conquering procrastination.

7.3. Negative Reinforcement and Procrastination

In contrast to positive reinforcement, negative reinforcement involves the removal of an unpleasant stimulus as a reward for a certain behavior. Think of the sweet relief that washes over you when you finally submit a project you've been delaying—the removal of that looming stress acts as negative reinforcement.

To harness the power of negative reinforcement, identify scenarios or factors that bring about feelings of discomfort in association with procrastination, such as stress, guilt, or anxiety. By actively addressing and then eliminating these adverse aspects, you're likely to create a natural inclination towards productivity.

7.4. The Role of Punishment in Behavior Modification

Punishment, in behavioral psychology, refers to the introduction of an aversive stimulus or the removal of a rewarding one to discourage certain behaviors. In the context of procrastination, it may initially seem counterintuitive to impose punishment on oneself. In fact, for effective behavior change, it is crucial to consider the role of punishment as a method of last resort and not the go-to strategy.

If procrastination persists despite your best efforts, you might need to introduce a form of mild self-imposed punishment. For instance, if you find yourself wasting too much time on social media instead of working, a good disciplinary step would be to temporarily deactivate your social media accounts until the work is completed.

Again, like with positive reinforcement, the key lies in balance; the punishment must not be too severe or have damaging effects. It must act as a deterrent against procrastination, not mental wellbeing.

7.5. Employing Behavioral Techniques for Long-Term Change

While each technique outlined above presents a potential pathway to overcoming procrastination, effective and lasting change lies in an individualized, holistic approach. Different factors drive procrastination for each person, meaning a diverse set of strategies might be necessary to combat it effectively.

Try out different techniques, be patient with yourself, and observe what works best for you. By viewing this journey as a process of self-discovery and growth rather than a daunting task, you're well on your way to breaking free from the shackles of procrastination.

Remember, change is steady but gradual – it might seem intimidating at first, but the rewards are tremendous. On the brighter side, each small step towards mastering these behavioral techniques is, in itself, a victory over procrastination. Continue pushing forward, experiment with different methodologies, and let the process of learning and growth mold you into a more productive version of yourself.

In this fight against procrastination, every individual has ample reserves of willpower and resilience at their disposal. With the understanding of behavioral techniques and their proficient employment, you have the power to break down the formidable walls of procrastination and step into the realm of productivity, organizing your life according to your terms. Employ these techniques, and allow emancipation from procrastination to guide you towards unparalleled efficiency and success.

Remember, the journey to conquering procrastination is not just about crossing off items on a to-do list, but about reclaiming your power to seize the day, attain your potential, and ultimately live a life of freedom, effectiveness, and satisfaction. Pave your path with persistence, reinforcement, and behavioral techniques and witness the remarkable transformation from procrastination to productivity!

Chapter 8. Maximizing Time Management: Tools and Techniques

Dipping our toes into the variegated world of productivity, the theme of time management naturally greets us as the first stepping stone. Time, the invincibly formidable yet remarkably gentle river, graciously invites us into its depth, offering a glimpse into infinite possibilities and elusive limitations. Under its wings, every tick of the clock carries immense potential. To capitalize on this potential, we must accumulate an impressive list of tools and techniques. It is time, dear reader, to embark on the journey toward maximizing time management.

8.1. The Principle of Time Boxing

One of the most effective tools in our productivity arsenal is Time Boxing. This is a strategic decision to allocate a fixed duration to a specific task, creating a 'box' around it. Essentially, you plan your day (or week) into a series of boxes, each one enclosing a standalone task. This technique is particularly useful for breaking down larger tasks into manageable 'chunks,' thereby preventing any feelings of overwhelm while boosting feelings of accomplishment and progress. Various digital tools, such as Google Calendar and Outlook, offer features that facilitate time boxing, while traditional pen-and-paper planners hold their rustic charm too.

8.2. The Power of Breaks: The Pomodoro Technique

Refining the time-boxing methodology further, we encounter a tomato-shaped clock that has revolutionized work ethos around the globe: The Pomodoro Technique. Named after the tide timer used by the technique's developer, the idea is simple: work with utmost intensity for 25 minutes, followed by a well-deserved 5-minute break. These intervals, known as 'pomodoros,' help redefine work cycles, offer requisite rest, and greatly reduce the discounting delay associated with finally beginning a dreaded task. Moreover, it enhances focus, encourages engagement, and fosters healthy work-life balance. Tools like TomatoTimer or Focus Keeper can serve as your personal Pomodoro timer, fostering an invigorating rhythm.

8.3. Prioritizing with Pareto Principle and Eisenhower Box

Directing our attention to the world of economics reveals another powerful tool: The Pareto Principle, or the 80/20 rule. This surmises that 80 percent of our outcomes come from just 20 percent of our efforts. By identifying and focusing on this vital 20 percent, we can significantly boost efficiency and productivity. Meanwhile, the Eisenhower Box helps prioritize tasks based on their urgency and importance. Dividing tasks into these four categories: urgent and important, not urgent but important, urgent but not important, and not urgent and not important, can help in deciding which tasks to do now, which to schedule for later, which to delegate, and which to remove altogether.

8.4. Embracing Technology: Digital Tools and Applications

With the digital age at its zenith, various software applications and platforms have emerged as saviors in the realm of productivity. Agile project management tools like Trello, productivity apps like TickTick, and efficient note-taking tools like OneNote and Evernote, all offer unique features for managing tasks, setting reminders, sharing work, and collaborating. Additionally, various time-tracking tools, such as RescueTime, allow for thorough self-assessments, pinpointing areas of time wastage and opportunities for efficiency.

8.5. Mindful Living: Meditation, Exercise, and Healthy Eating

Delving into holistic living, it's invaluable to mention the role of mindfulness, physical exercise, and a nutritious diet in enhancing time management. A calm mind can process tasks faster and with more accuracy, leading to better time utilization. Guided meditation apps like Headspace and Calm are great tools for fostering mindfulness. Incorporating regular physical activity and a wholesome diet can drastically improve your mental clarity, concentration, energy levels, and overall well-being, leading to a more efficient use of your time.

As we wrap up this chapter, it's essential to realize that effective time management is not merely about the mechanistic lining up of tasks and schedules. It lies equally in fostering a healthier, more mindful lifestyle that nourishes your mind, body, and spirit. After all, as Seneca quipped, "It's not that we have little time, but more that we waste a good deal of it." The tools and techniques mentioned here will set you off on a compassionate journey to reclaim your time and direct it toward tasks that truly matter, marking a significant stride in your transition from procrastination to productivity. These sophisticated techniques not only maximize your productivity, they also create opportunities to break free from stress and enjoy life to the fullest.

Chapter 9. Becoming an Efficiency Expert: Practical Approaches

The transition from an overwhelmed procrastinator into an efficiency expert is not an overnight stance but occurs incrementally. It is an exciting and fulfilling journey that can be mapped out in practical steps; outlined by researched-based strategies coupled with effective approaches that you can apply in everyday situations to defeat procrastination. This transformational process involves a series of essential elements geared towards increasing your productivity and improving your time management.

9.1. Deconstructing Tasks into Manageable Units

It is not uncommon to procrastinate big tasks; their large scope and extensive requirements often seem too overwhelming, causing delay. The solution is to break down these tasks into smaller, manageable units. This deconstruction might mean subdividing a task into stages based on the required steps or resources needed. This process reduces the perceived enormity and difficulty of the task at hand, making it less intimidating and inviting action over delay. By conquering these smaller tasks one at a time, you can progressively accomplish the whole task.

For example, if you're tasked with preparing an annual report, break it down into smaller tasks such as research, data analysis, writing the report, proofreading, and final reviews. What seemed insurmountable at first now seems achievable, fuelling motivation towards completion and inching you closer towards becoming an efficiency expert.

9.2. Harnessing the Power of Technology

In an age where technology continues to grow and evolve, it's imperative to leverage these tools to improve your efficiency. There are numerous applications and platforms designed to manage tasks, tracking progress, and measuring productivity. Explore tools like Asana, Trello, or Todoist for task management, or RescueTime for tracking where your time goes. Digital calendars, like Google Calendar or Microsoft Outlook, could also be instrumental in managing your time effectively.

Adopting these technologies in your daily routine can streamline your tasks, improve your efficiency, and help monitor your progress. The key is to find what works best for you and make it a part of your habits. Remember that these tools are meant to serve as enablers; they're only as useful as your commitment to use them effectively.

9.3. Prioritizing Tasks Effectively

Equally important to breaking down tasks is the ability to prioritize them. Prioritizing your tasks removes the confusion and haphazardness that often come with a giant to-do list. Employing systems like the Eisenhower Matrix, which categorizes tasks into four quadrants based on their urgency and importance, can be instrumental.

This system helps you identify critical and noncritical tasks, as well as distinguish between tasks that require immediate attention and those that can wait. By doing this, you not only work on what's important at any given time but also avoid wasting time on trivial tasks. Prioritizing tasks is an essential skill to becoming an efficiency expert as it reduces inefficiencies and mismanagement, promoting productivity and time optimization.

9.4. Adopting Effective Time Management Techniques

In your journey towards efficiency proficiency, time management techniques such as the Pomodoro technique or time blocking can be particularly useful. The Pomodoro technique, for example, stipulates working for a specified time, usually 25 minutes, focusing entirely on the task at hand followed by a 5-minute break. This pattern helps maintain focus and productivity levels without leading to burnout.

Time blocking, on the other hand, involves scheduling specific times in your day for particular tasks or activities. This method can help prevent distractions and interruptions that inhibit productivity and contribute to procrastination. Additionally, time blocking can encourage a sense of discipline and maximization of time usage.

9.5. Developing and Maintaining a Positive Mindset

While techniques and strategies play a significant role in becoming an efficiency expert, your mindset is just as important. Maintaining positivity and motivation can significantly impact your ability to combat procrastination and become an efficiency expert. Overcoming challenges and persevering in times of adversity requires mental resilience and self-encouragement.

To further harness the power of a positive mindset, consider adopting mindfulness techniques. Mindfulness can assist in reducing stress, improving focus, and promoting mental clarity, all central components to enhanced productivity. Practice regular meditation, mindful breaks, and engage in mindful activities to strengthen your resilience and foster a productivity-oriented mindset.

9.6. Creating a Conducive Work Environment

Finally, your environment impacts your efficiency significantly. Set up a neat, distraction-free space that stimulates productivity and minimizes interruptions, giving you the opportunity to focus solely on your tasks. Use ergonomically-friendly furniture to avoid physical discomfort and fatigue. If possible, personalize your workspace with elements that promote positivity and motivation, like plants or motivational quotes.

Transitioning from procrastination to productivity is a journey, an ongoing process that requires consistency, discipline, and persistence. But with the right tools, techniques, and mindset, you are well on your way to becoming an efficiency expert. And remember, every step taken towards this goal is a step away from procrastination and a stride towards a more fulfilled, productive life.

Chapter 10. Maintaining Productivity Momentum: Avoiding Backslide

The last stretch of the journey towards total productivity conquest is as essential as the first. You've embarked on the trip, cruised through various terrain, and finally, you're here. As the glow of initial success begins to wane, it is pivotal not to backslide into old procrastination habits. This chapter will explore how to maintain your productivity momentum, focusing on strategies for avoiding backslide, ensuring that your association with procrastination remains a thing of the past, thus transforming you into a consistent, efficient, and productive individual.

10.1. The Concept and Importance of Momentum

Understanding momentum is the first step to maintaining your hard-won productivity surge. In simplest terms, momentum refers to the impetus gained by a moving object. Applying the concept to productivity, it's the forward motion you've gained through consistently adhering to productive habits. This momentum is your surest bet for avoiding backslide. The more substantial your momentum, the harder it is for old habits to creep back in and derail your progress.

Productivity momentum is about stringing together successful days, weeks, and months. It's fueled by consistency, discipline, and motivation, all of which maintain the positive energy necessary for achieving your long-term goals.

10.2. Strategies to Keep the Momentum Going

To keep the productivity momentum going, here are several strategies that can keep you on course, and prevent any unwelcome return of procrastination habits.

10.2.1. Positive Reinforcement

Rewarding yourself after completion of tasks can reinforce the positive behavior. Whether it's an extra few minutes of relaxation, a tasty snack, or indulging in a hobby, giving yourself rewards can boost motivation and make you more likely to keep up with beneficial behavior patterns.

10.2.2. Regular Evaluation and Tracking Your Progress

Keeping track of your progress is a powerful way to maintain momentum. Seeing your accomplishments quantified can provide the much-needed motivation to push forward. Use digital tools and apps designed for productivity to keep tabs on your tasks, time allocation, and completed goals.

10.2.3. Adopt A Growth Mindset

Those who believe in their ability to grow and improve are the ones who do. Embrace the reality that you're bound to face challenges along the way, but resist the urge to see these as insurmountable obstacles. Instead, view them as opportunities for growth, and use them to refine and strengthen your productivity strategies.

10.2.4. Taking Purposeful Breaks

Breaks are crucial in avoiding burnout and sustaining momentum. Studies show that people who take regular, intentional breaks maintain higher levels of focus, creativity, and productivity than those who push through without rest.

10.2.5. Seek Feedback

Feedback from colleagues, mentors, or peers is invaluable for continuous learning, growth, and maintaining momentum. Constructive feedback can shed light on areas that need adjustment or improvement, preventing you from getting stuck in a feedback loop.

10.3. Bouncing Back from Slip-ups: The Art of Resilience

Even with all these strategies, there will still be times when you falter. Productivity is about progress, not perfection. The real measure of success isn't about never falling but in the ability to get up each time you fall.

In these moments, practicing self-compassion is essential. Acknowledge the slip-up, learn from it, and use what you've learned to spur you forward. Developing resilience allows you to bounce back speedily rather than wallow in self-pity or frustration.

Keep in mind the importance of reinforcing positive habits and mechanisms, regular self-evaluation, adopting a growth mindset, taking purposeful breaks, and seeking feedback. These, coupled with a resilient spirit, bolster your momentum, keeping procrastination at bay, and ensuring your achievements are lasting.

In conclusion, maintaining productivity momentum and avoiding backslide isn't a one-off action, but a continuous process that demands vigilance, self-awareness, and a relentless desire for self-improvement. Embed these strategies into your routine, and your journey to conquer procrastination becomes not just a chapter in your life, but a sustainable, lifelong narrative. No longer will you be locked in a battle with time, but instead, you will master it, becoming the efficiency powerhouse you've always aspired to be.

Chapter 11. Turning a New Leaf: Your Future Free of Procrastination

In the previous stages of our journey, we have acknowledged the insidious nature of procrastination, established its core psychological factors, recognized time as our most precious resource, delved into the complex dynamics of human behavior and habit formation, shifted from the grips of procrastination to the controls of productivity, employed efficacious behavioral techniques to combat procrastination, harnessed the prowess of time management tools and techniques, and adopted practical approaches of an efficiency expert. It is now time to secure your newly acquired status as a productivity adept, shielding it from potential backslides, and foresee a future free from the talons of procrastination. This pivotal chapter aims to provide you with exhaustive instruction on how to prudently cast off the shackles of procrastination and embrace your ascendance to a more efficient and productive future.

11.1. Nurturing the Productivity Powerhouse

Enhance your newfound proficiency by focusing not merely on the elimination of procrastination, but by instilling a deep-seated productive mindset. You will apprehend key philosophies, which will empower you to continually foster and nourish your productivity prowess.

11.2. Cultivating Resilience Amidst Setbacks

Setbacks are inevitable and can pose a sizable threat to our progress. As such, it's crucial to build effective resilience strategies to counteract these potential hindrances. Understanding how to maintain morale, stay focused, and regroup when faced with setbacks, will ensure the continuation of your productivity journey without succumbing to the lurking procrastination.

11.3. Guarding Against Procrastination Relapse

Inclinations toward old ways can still emerge, even after significant productivity growth. Here, we will explore advanced tactics for fortifying your resistance against a potential procrastination relapse, which includes monitoring progress, mindfulness practices, and refining your self-management repertoire continually.

11.4. The Power of Consistency

For the long-term maintenance of productivity, consistency is an invaluable trait. Incorporating it into your daily habits and routines is a determining factor in sustaining your momentum. We will delve further into how consistency can be reinforced by touching base with our goals daily and structuring routines that accommodate our natural rhythms and proclivities.

11.5. Embracing Agility: Adapting Your Strategies

Just as our circumstances are ever-changing, our strategies should be dynamic enough to evolve accordingly. You'll acquire skills to gauge when a productivity strategy requires modification or replacement, ensuring your productivity toolkit remains relevant and effective.

11.6. Envisioning a Procrastination-Free Future

Finally, we will envision the future that you desire - a future free from the debilitating effects of procrastination. You will learn to manifest this vision into reality by implementing goal-setting techniques, avowing future-focused self-talk, and persistently celebrating productivity wins, no matter how small, through positive reinforcement.

In sum, this chapter is all about preserving the progress you've made so far, and preparing for a future where procrastination has no hold over you, allowing you to truly own your time, optimize productivity, and live life on your terms. Let this journey to turning a new leaf unfurl into a lifelong evolution of growth, gratification, and success, which you truly deserve. Keep this grand future in sight, hold firm to your tools, skills, and strategies you've cultivated, and welcome the promising dawn free from the clutches of procrastination.

www.ingramcontent.com/pod-product-compliance
Lightning Source LLC
Chambersburg PA
CBHW070942220526
45469CB00007B/2488